THE PSALMS AND PRAYERS OF JOSEPH

VOL. # 1

BY: JOSEPH ALLEN ASHE, SR.

The Psalms and Prayers of Joseph - Vol. #1

By: Joseph Allen Ashe, Sr.

Cover Design by: Andre M. Saunders
Logo Design by: Andre M. Saunders
Photography by: Photobucket
Editor: Alisha Broughton
Associate Editor: Anelda L. Ballard

© 2009 Joseph Allen Ashe, Sr.

ISBN 978-0-9768540-8-1
ISBN 0-9768540-8-2

All rights reserved. This book is protected under the copyright laws of the United States of America. This book may not be copied or reprinted for commercial gain or profit. The use of short quotations or occasional page copying for personal or group study is permitted and encouraged. Permission will be granted upon request.

Scripture quotations are taken from the Maxwell Leadership Bible, King James Version, New King James Version, New International Version and the New Living Translation of the Holy Bible.

For Worldwide Distribution
Printed in the United States of America
Published by Jazzy Kitty Greetings Marketing & Publishing, LLC
Utilizing Adobe and Microsoft Publishing Software

ACKNOWLEDGMENTS

I first give thanks to God because God is my everything. Without God, I would have no talent. Without God, this book could not be. Therefore, I give to God all of the credit.

DEDICATIONS

I dedicate this book to the three people that I love the most: Jelisa Andrea Dixon, Tanesha Lanae' Dixon, and Joseph Allen Ashe Jr. They are all my babies and I wish that I could have been a much better father to them.

I'd also like to thank and recognize Chaplain Charles Jolwan (Chaplain Charlie) and family. Chaplain was the Spiritual Leader and Minister at Gander Hill Prison. He was also my best friend and my role model. He passed away a few years ago. Before he died, Chaplain prophesied to me saying, "When Joe Ashe gets himself together, he's going to be a millionaire."

Also I would like to thank Pastor Veronice Horne and every member of Holy Hands Worship Center in Newark, New Jersey. You've truly been my backbone. I would like to thank Ms. Rosalynn Boddy for her never failing, unconditional love, and support. She's my sister and my friend. I like to thank Rev. Dr. George W. Bratcher, Jr. (my cousin) for his time, love, support, and dedication. George is the man who pulled me off the streets when I was homeless. I love you, George.

To Mildred Bernice Christy-Ashe, you were my mother. You were the best. When God took you, a major part of me was taken also. You were always right. I'm sorry for all of the times that I disappointed you, let you down, hurt your feelings, frustrated you, or chose to be everything but the son that you worked so hard to raise. At least today, I know that you would be proud.

To Rev. Joseph McDonald Ashe (my father), I'm sorry for all of the times that I let you down and I pray that you can someday find it in your heart to forgive me. I've already forgiven you and I've asked God to forgive you as well. I wish you well in life and in your ministry.

DEDICATIONS

To Jennie Virginia Ashe (my wife), I want you to know I'm sorry for all of the bad times in our marriage. You are truly a good woman. Thank you for believing in me when no one else would. I pray that you forgive me, as I have forgiven you. May God touch your heart. May God rain blessings down upon you, and may He keep you in all situations and circumstances.

To Jesus Christ (My Lord, My Savior, and My Everything), although your name comes last, You are truly first. Without You, nothing would be possible. This book belongs to You, My Lord.

TABLE OF CONTENTS

Introduction..	i
Prayer For The Book...	2
It All Belongs To God..	3
A Friend...	5
If You Are In Christ...	6
What Should I Do?..	7
What Jesus Does...	9
Good Father..	10
I'll Keep You First..	11
I'm Sorry..	13
Keep Pushing..	14
Just A Child...	15
He Loves Me..	17
No Man..	19
A Solid Prayer..	21
Take My Life..	22
Could Be Worse...	23
On The Shelf..	25
I'm Ready..	27
Baptism..	29
Changed...	31
Mold Me...	33

TABLE OF CONTENTS

Use Me..	34
No Worries...	35
Believe It..	37
Right On Time...	38
A Voice...	39
Nourishment..	41
Be Careful..	42
Stop Forgetting...	43
Give It To God...	45
Standing There...	46
It Can Be Fixed..	47
Prayer Is Your Defense..	49
Write A Letter To God.......................................	51
Struggling..	53
He's Real..	54
Hypocrite...	55
Someday...	57
Nobody Told Me..	58
Be Patient..	60
Bless My Home..	62
Are You Planted?...	65
A Brother...	67

TABLE OF CONTENTS

One Answer	68
Saved	70
I'm Desperate	71
I'm Going to Talk to God	73
He Can	74
Me	75
Call On Jesus	76
Morning Prayer	78
Preparation	79
It's All Good	80
Thank you, Lord	81
Thanks	82

INTRODUCTION

God has blessed me with the talent to write and recite poetry. This book contains my personal prayers, thoughts, and beliefs. Every poem that I have written has a powerful message. My goal is to pass that message on to those who believe and read my book. Each poem paints its own picture. God's strength is perfect. Prayer changes everything. Trust in the Lord and talk to Him.

This book is just one example of how God can use someone as His vessel to bring forth His personal messages. I was broke, homeless, and strung out on drugs. God delivered me and through these poems He healed me. Today, I am free of any type of substances. I don't drink alcohol, I don't smoke cigarettes, and I am no longer homeless. My whole life has changed.

Open up your heart and your mind as you read my poetry. Then let God work miracles in your life. May God bless each and every reader. If God can change me, He can change anyone. May you read, enjoy, and prosper.

PRAYER FOR THIS BOOK

LORD, I GIVE YOU THE GLORY RIGHT NOW. I PRAY FOR BLESSINGS, FOR THOSE WHO READ MY STORIES.

PRAYER FOR THIS BOOK

Lord, I've learned to listen.
Lord, I've learned to pray.
Lord, in everything I do,
I want You to have your way.

Lord, I'm working on obedience;
I'm trying hard to stay humble.
Lord, by building my life on You,
No longer will I trip, fall, or stumble.

Lord, I give You my time;
Lord, I give You the Glory!
Right now, I pray for blessings;
For those who read my stories.

Lord, if it's Your will,
Then let Your will be done.
In Jesus' Name, let these words I write,
TOUCH THE MINDS AND HEARTS OF EVERYONE!

IT ALL BELONGS TO GOD

God is the One who created me,

I do not belong to myself.

I should only be concerned about doing God's will,

Not with the thoughts of someone else.

My life is not my life,

For it truly belongs to Jesus.

The One who sacrificed His life,

In order for Him to free us.

My body is not my body,

It is a temple of the Lord.

Everything that goes inside,

I must be careful to thank Him for.

I must continuously give Him praise.

I must thank Him because I know,

That everything belongs to Him;

FROM MY HEAD, DOWN TO MY TOE!

A FRIEND

HE IS THE SON OF GOD, BORN OF THE VIRGIN MARY. HE SHED HIS BLOOD ON A RUGGED CROSS.

A FRIEND

I thought I had good friends,
Until I was told about this Guy;
Who gave His life for me one day.
His story made me cry!

He is the Son of God,
Born of the Virgin Mary.
He shed His blood on a rugged cross,
He died, then He was buried.

He made a promise to everyone,
That He would come back again.
He suffered this painful death,
That we may be forgiven of our sins.

Three days after His death;
This Man was alive and walking.
He had scars from being on the cross,
He had a glow and He was talking.

He cared so much about me,
This Man shed His blood.
Now, I'm sure that I have a Friend,
JUST LOOK AT HOW HE PROVED HIS LOVE.

IF YOU ARE IN CHRIST

If you are in Christ,

You are a fisher of men.

Your mission is to lead those,

Who are living in sin.

Do not be afraid,

God will surely protect you.

Teach the Word of God,

To anyone you can get to.

You are a disciple,

A leader in Christ.

Tell the world about the gift

Of everlasting life!

I'll tell you right now,

Some people that you meet;

May refuse the Word of God.

Just shake the dust off your feet!

If you try to talk to many;

Yet, you only lead one.

Teach him about Christ;

AND, THE MIRACLES THAT HE'S DONE!

WHAT SHOULD I DO?

Lord, I really need You;

My mind is real confused.

Although my heart knows right from wrong,

It's hard for me to choose.

Sometimes I am tempted,

Yet, I try to wait on You.

Knowing that You are the only One,

Who really knows what to do.

I need to hear Your voice,

At least send me a sign.

A hint of which way I should go,

To help make up my mind.

Lord, please be my eyes;

Be my heart and be my brain.

Lord, You know the answers;

PLEASE HELP ME, IN JESUS' NAME!

WHAT JESUS DOES

I DECIDED TO BELIEVE AND STARTED PRAYING. TODAY, I READ MY BIBLE AND TRY TO LIVE BY WHAT IT'S SAYING.

WHAT JESUS DOES

I used to be a man on drugs,
I really didn't know who Christ was.
I use to lie, I use to cheat, and I use to steal;
I've committed adultery and I've even tried to kill.

I've been aggressive, abusive, and drunk;
I've used language so dirty, it stunk!
I've displayed so many sinful behaviors;
I've shown hate to my brother and my neighbors.

Just when I believed that I couldn't change,
Into my life, a Man named Jesus came!
I begged Him to forgive my sins,
He said, "Only if you believe that I can."

I decided to believe and started praying,
Today, I read my Bible and try to live by what it's saying.
I'm no longer the man that I was,
I'M LIVING PROOF OF WHAT JESUS DOES!

GOOD FATHER

Lord, I love my children;
I want to be in their lives.
Lord, I love my children;
I want to be great in their eyes.

I want to be their friend,
And, give them what they need.
Help me to be an example,
Please help me Lord to lead.

Help me to show them love,
To teach them all respect.
Help me to teach the Word of God,
So they won't have to guess.

I want to be a father,
The best that I can be.
Lord, for all of my children's sake;
PLEASE MAKE A BETTER ME!

I'LL KEEP YOU FIRST

Lord, I'll keep You first;
In my words and in my ways.
Lord, I'll keep You first;
I'll give You the highest praise!

Lord, I'll keep You first;
I love You with all of my heart!
Lord, I'll keep You first,
Because of who You are.

Lord, I'll keep You first;
I'll pray in Jesus' Name.
Lord, I'll keep You first;
My life won't be the same.

Lord, I'll keep You first;
I'll sing a song to You.
Lord, I'll keep You first;
IN EVERYTHING THAT I DO!

I'M SORRY

TODAY I ASK FORGIVENESS, I CANNOT APOLOGIZE ENOUGH. LORD, PLEASE TELL ME WHAT I CAN DO TO TRY TO MAKE THIS UP.

I'M SORRY!

I'M SORRY

Today I cried,
Something was taken...You see.
Something that I had done for God;
Just because He loves me.

Today my heart is mourning,
I feel like I let God down.
I should have been more careful,
Maybe it wouldn't have been found.

Today God, I am sorry;
That I have disappointed You.
I feel like a knife was put to my heart,
And, someone slowly pushed it through.

Today I ask forgiveness,
I can not apologize enough!
Lord, please tell me what I can do,
To try to make this up.

I'M SORRY!

KEEP PUSHING

Every time I take two steps,
Three steps gets taken way.
Every time I turn around,
My life is on delay.

It's meant for me to reach the top;
Yet, I keep falling as I climb.
I get close enough to see my goal,
Then I fall on my behind!

I can't let myself get tired.
I can't let myself give up;
At times, I get discouraged;
Yet, I can't let myself get stuck.

I'm pushing Lord, I'm pushing Lord;
With everything that I've got!
I'm giving You my everything,
Although it's not a lot.

I'm trusting in Your promises,
I'm leaning on Your Word.
One day, I'll get what I'm striving for;
DESPITE THE FALLS THAT OCCURRED.

JUST A CHILD

I am just a child;
I pray to God every night.

I am just a child;
I believe in Jesus, The Christ.

I am just a child;
God help me to be patient.

I am just a child;
I am one of Your creations.

I am just a child;
I'm learning to do right.

I am just a child;
I am precious in God's sight.

I am just a child;
I love God with all of my might!

I am just a child;
PROTECTED BY JESUS CHRIST!

HE LOVES ME

YOU ARE JUST SO GREAT, YOU KEEP GIVING ME SO MUCH. I THANK YOU LORD, I LIFT UP YOUR NAME; I CAN'T PRAISE YOU ENOUGH.

HE LOVES ME

I just can't help myself,
I need to give You praise.
For You have been my everything;
Showing me love in many ways.

My God, My God...I can't say enough,
You keep supplying all my needs.
You gave me life, You keep me fed;
You give me the air to breathe.

You are just so great,
You keep giving me so much.
I thank you Lord, I lift up Your name;
I can't praise You enough.

You sacrificed Your Son,
He died on Calvary.
What greater way for anyone to show…
HIS LOVE FOR ME!

NO MAN

EVEN IF A MAN WAS STRONGER THAN AN OX AND TALLER THAN ANY TREE. WHATEVER IS IN GOD'S PLAN, NO MAN CAN TAKE FROM ME.

NO MAN

A man can think what he wants,
He can plot and scheme all day.
Yet, whatever God has chosen for me,
No man can take it away!

Try to argue, fuss, or fight,
In fact, give me your best shot.
In the end, you'll find, my Friend,
You can't have what I've got.

You can try to use a weapon,
You can bring with you an army.
You still won't get what I got from God,
Plus, God won't let you harm me!

Even if a man was stronger than an ox,
And, taller than any tree;
Whatever is in God's plan,
NO MAN CAN TAKE FROM ME!

A SOLID PRAYER

LORD, TAKE ME IN YOUR ARMS; DO WITH ME, AS YOU MAY. LORD, PLEASE CONTINUE TO BLESS ME;

IN JESUS' NAME, I PRAY.

A SOLID PRAYER

Lord, forgive me for my sins;
Each day I come short.
Lord, give me strength and courage;
In hopes that I can endure.

Lord, lead me through this day;
Guide my steps as You will.
Lord, cover me from head to my toe;
Protecting me with Your shield.

Lord, keep me safe and healthy;
Humble my thoughts, give me peace.
Lord, continue to provide for me;
All of the things that I need.

Lord, give me knowledge and understanding;
Mold me in Your Word.
Lord, give me wisdom and obedience;
To stay straight and never swerve.

Lord, take me in Your arms;
Do with me, as You may.
Lord, please continue to bless me;
IN JESUS' NAME, I PRAY.

TAKE MY LIFE

Lord, please take my life;
I'm asking for another chance.
Lord, please take my life;
I'm putting it in Your hands.

Lord, please take my life;
Mold me, just like clay.
Lord, please take my life;
Keep me from going astray.

Lord, please take my life;
My back is against the ropes.
Lord, please take my life;
You are my only hope.

Lord, please take my life;
Forgive me I'm a sinner.
Lord, please take my life;
In You, I'll be a winner.

Lord, please take my life;
I need You right away.
Lord, please take my life;
IN JESUS' NAME, I PRAY!

COULD BE WORSE

At times, I struggle to pay my bills;
My wife and I may have disputes.
My children don't always act right,
At times I get confused.

At times, a family member is sick.
At times, I don't feel well myself.
At times, I just can't get it together.
At times, I desperately need help.

At times, life may seem hectic;
Something always goes wrong.
I've never seen a perfect day,
God, I ask You, Please keep me strong!

I stare out at the world,
I must keep giving God the praise.
My life is not the greatest,
YET, I HAVE SEEN WORSE DAYS.

ON THE SHELF

ALL ALONG, I HAD THE ANSWERS;
YET, MY BIBLE WAS ON THE SHELF!

ON THE SHELF

Today I am angry,
I do not know why?
Although my heart cries,
Tears fall not from my eyes.

I don't want to be touched,
I don't want to be spoken to.
I'm upset with the world,
I have no clue what to do.

I don't want to be alone,
I am not in my right mind.
I'll just pray to God,
For the answers that I can't find.

No longer will I be angry,
Just disappointed in myself.
All along, I had the answers;
Yet, my Bible was on the shelf.

(Continued)

ON THE SHELF

God will let me go through things,
If I forget to put Him first.
Prolonging to give it to God,
Makes my problems worse.

He already knows my every need,
I must put trust in Him.
Believing that He is the answer,
To each and every problem.

The Bible is filled with God's Word,
Yet, I kept it on the shelf.
I had no reason to be upset,
JUST ANGRY, WITH MYSELF!

I'M READY

I feel like I'm ready Lord,
Yet, is it really my time?
I've given You my everything,
You know my heart, You know my mind.

Lord, I'm not in trouble;
I'm stepping out on faith.
It's time for me to spread my wings,
Tell me, if I'm making a mistake.

Lord, You know that I love You;
I need You, can't You see?
I need a job, I need a place of my own;
Will You open these doors for me?

I want this to be Your will,
I need Your blessings upon this.
I'm begging You Lord, for prosperity;
Please, take me inside Your fist.

Lord, You said, "If I ask,
Then I can consider it done."
Lord, I ask this blessing;
IN THE NAME OF CHRIST, YOUR SON

BAPTISM

I WENT DOWN IN THE WATER, SUBMERGED FROM HEAD TO TOE. A BRAND NEW LIFE IN CHRIST, A NEWBORN THAT'S READY TO GROW.

Matthew 3:11
Baptism signifies repentance.

BAPTISM

I went down in the water,
Submerged from head to toe.
A brand new life in Christ,
A newborn that's ready to grow.

I took all of my wrongful doings,
Every sin and sinful thought.
I buried them in that water,
I came up with a clean new chart.

This baptism meant everything to me;
Before it started, I got on my knees.
I cried, "Dear God, I repent, I repent!"
"Forgive me for everything, please!"

It wasn't about my church,
It wasn't about my friends.
I wanted to do this right,
I didn't want to leave any loose strings.

(Continued)

BAPTISM

Dear God, It was all about You;
I have chosen to give You my life.
I know I'll have a room in Your mansion,
If You choose to take me tonight.

I believe, I believe, I believe;
I've been saved, I've been saved, I've been saved!
I love You, I love You, I love You;
I give You praise, I give You praise, I give You praise!

CHANGED

Today, I have my ups and downs;
Tomorrow I have hope.
I'm standing on God's promises,
The promises that He wrote.

It's all about God's Word,
We must read, study, and obey.
Take everything that's on our mind,
Get down on our knees and pray.

I've learned to talk to God,
I love Him, He's my Friend;
Through Christ who strengthens me,
I know I can, I know I can!

Everyday may be a struggle,
Yet, I can smile because I have joy.
Before my life in Christ,
I was one of Satan's toys.

Dear God, I lift You up;
Dear God, I praise Your name;
I thank You Lord,
BECAUSE OF YOU MY WHOLE LIFE HAS CHANGED!

MOLD ME

YOU ARE MY POTTER, I AM YOUR CLAY. PROTECT ME LORD, WHILE YOU TEACH ME; MOLD ME IN YOUR WAY.

MOLD ME

I'm changing Lord, I'm changing;
You are my potter, I am Your clay.
Protect me Lord, while You teach me;
Mold me in Your way!

I'm learning Lord, I'm learning;
You are my Teacher and my Friend.
Give me knowledge and understanding,
As much as You possibly can.

I'm ready Lord, I'm ready;
Please guide my every step.
Help me if I begin to swerve;
Please, do not let me wreck!

I'm willing Lord, I'm willing;
To follow You all the way.
I need You Lord, I need You;
IN JESUS' NAME, I PRAY!

USE ME

Place Your shield upon me Lord,
Protect me from Satan's ways.
Only You can guide my steps,
Only You deserve to be praised.

Lord, give me strength and courage.
I am only one,
Unworthy of the Blood of Jesus;
Christ Your only Son.

Have Your way in me, Oh Lord;
That my light may shine bright.
So that others may see You in me,
Believe and receive eternal life.

Dear God, I am Your soldier;
Though weary as I can be.
Allow me to be Your vessel Lord,
I AM YOURS, "PLEASE USE ME!"

NO WORRIES

Nobody seems to understand me,
I feel that I'm severely disliked.
I was loved when I was doing wrong,
I'm hated, because I'm doing right.

I ask you all to keep me in prayer,
This road that I'm walking is tough.
Satan is angry because I'm serving God,
I guess that's why everything is rough.

I'm trying real hard to stay humble,
Daily I'm put to the test.
Sometimes, I am weak and I slip;
God knows that I'm trying my best.

I'm not going to sit back and worry.
There is one thing for sure that I've learned;
This world in time may come to hate me.
YET, CHRIST IS MY ONLY CONCERN.

BELIEVE IT

IF I WANT IT, I CAN HAVE IT.
IF I BELIEVE IT, THEN IT'S MINE!

SOMETIMES I HAVE TO BE PATIENT, KNOWING THAT GOD IS ALWAYS ON TIME.

BELIEVE IT

Nobody said, "It would be easy."
Yet, I'm stepping out on faith.
Although I believe in Jesus Christ,
I'm still going to make mistakes.

Prayer is my defense,
Against the Wicked One.
My perfect chance to talk to God;
And, thank Him for what He's done.

I have to keep my head up,
I have to keep marching on.
God is good; God is great;
God will keep me strong!

If I want it, I can have it.
If I believe it, then it's mine!
Sometimes I have to be patient,
Knowing that God is always on time.

God is just so good!
I can be what I want to be.
Knowing that all things are possible,
THROUGH CHRIST WHO STRENGTHENS ME!

RIGHT ON TIME

Just when I thought that I couldn't;
You showed me that I could.
Just when I thought that I was bad,
You showed me, I could be good.

Just when I thought that I was a loser,
You showed me, I could win.
Just when I thought my life was gone,
You gave it back again.

Just when I thought I was hopeless,
You showed me, there was hope.
Just when I thought that I was lost,
You showed me which way to go.

Just when I thought that I was tired,
You gave me back my wind.
Just when I thought I was going to Hell,
You forgave me for my sins!

Just when I thought about giving up,
You took that thought from me.
Just when I thought that I was living in chains,
YOU CAME AND YOU SET ME FREE!

A VOICE

I hear a voice and it sounds familiar,
I hear a voice and it's calling my name.
I don't see a face; I just hear the voice;
Now this voice is racking my brain.

It's trying to tell me something;
In fact, it is saying to me, "Repent!"
The Kingdom of God is coming, it says,
"The return of the one God sent."

It's telling me to get right with God,
It's telling me not to wait.
It's telling me to believe and except Jesus Christ,
It's saying, "Hurry, before it's too late."

I hear it saying, "God will forgive you."
I hear it saying, "Turn from your ways."
It's telling me that I can have everlasting life,
It's telling me, that I can be saved.

Satan wants me dead,
This voice says, "You can live."
It's telling me that God will forgive me,
IF I REPENT, FOR EVERYTHING THAT I DID.

NOURISHMENT

MILK IS A GREAT SOURCE OF CALCIUM, IT'S GREAT FOR YOUR TEETH AND YOUR BONES. BUT, JESUS CHRIST IS THE GREATEST THING, FOR YOUR MIND, YOUR BODY, AND SOUL.

NOURISHMENT

Carrots are good for your eyes,
Beets are good for your blood.
Meat is a great source of protein,
I don't know what cabbage does.

Milk is a great source of calcium,
It's great for your teeth and your bones.
Grapefruit helps you to burn off fat,
Most people leave spinach alone.

Weights will build up your strength,
Exercise is good for your heart.
Studying expands your knowledge,
Reading is food for your thoughts.

The Bible tells us everything,
It's food that can't be put in a bowl.
Jesus Christ is the greatest thing,
FOR YOUR MIND, YOUR BODY, AND SOUL.

BE CAREFUL

Be careful of who you call your friend;
Be careful of who you call your leader.
Be careful of who is preaching to you;
Be careful of who you call your teacher.

Be careful of who may give you advice;
Be careful of who gives you a hand.
Be careful of who you're leaning on;
Be careful of who helps you to understand.

Be careful of who you hang around;
Be careful of who you are obeying.
Satan may come in any way, shape, or form…
BE CAREFUL, THAT'S ALL I'M SAYING!

STOP FORGETTING

Why am I worried?
Why is my life in disarray?
Did I forget to talk to God?
Did I forget to pray?

Why am I stressed out?
Why am I confused?
Did I forget the Bible,
Is the book that bears Good News?

Why am I depressed?
Why do I feel down?
Did I forget to give God praise?
He's standing here, right now!

Why am I unhappy?
Why can't I just smile?
God is good all of the time,
Not just once in a while.

Why am I not jumping around?
Screaming in Jesus' Name?
If I remember that my joy is in Christ,
ALL OF THESE FEELINGS WILL CHANGE.

GIVE IT TO GOD

I FIND THE STRENGTH TO GET ON MY KNEES, THEN, GIVE GOD A CALL.

GIVE IT TO GOD

In times of trouble,

When no one seems to care.

When everyone who I've called my friend,

Just cannot be there.

When the world is on my shoulders,

When I feel weak and in need of rest.

When I'm tired and just cannot take no more,

When too much weight is on my chest!

When life no longer matters,

When I'm ready to end it all.

I find the strength to get on my knees,

Then, give God a call.

No problem is too great for Him,

No weight He cannot bear.

If I call on God and believe,

IF I'M PATIENT HE WILL ANSWER MY PRAYERS.

STANDING THERE

Oh Lord, When I'm confused;
When I just don't understand.
When frustration seems to settle in,
When I can't figure out the plan.

When nobody knows what I'm talking about,
When things begin to seem blurry.
When I find myself starting to scratch my head,
When my focus turns into worry.

At times like this I believe that,
God is in the middle of planning.
The Bible says to Trust in the Lord,
I lean not unto my own understanding.

God knows everything,
I must remember to stay in prayer.
No matter how complicated things may get,
GOD WILL BE STANDING THERE.

IT CAN BE FIXED

Satan has stripped me down,
Yet, I can be rebuilt.
Satan has emptied me,
Yet, I can be refilled.

Satan has destroyed my hope,
Yet, my hopes are not a waste.
Satan has taken away my dreams,
Yet, they can be replaced.

Satan has crushed my spirit,
Yet, that can be restored.
Satan has ruined my chances,
Yet, I can still win this war.

Satan has had His way in me,
Yet, I can stop Him in His tracks.
Satan has taken away everything,
YET, GOD CAN GIVE IT BACK!

PRAYER IS YOUR DEFENSE

PRAYER CAN SOLVE WHATEVER IT IS THAT SATAN ATTEMPTS TO DO. PRAYER IS ALSO THE ONLY WAY THAT SATAN WILL FLEE FROM YOU!

PRAYER IS YOUR DEFENSE

I feel like I'm slipping,
Satan is pulling on me.
He knows that I'm in Christ,
He just refuses to flee.

I admit sometimes I'm weak,
Sometimes my prayer is delayed.
Although I trust and believe in Jesus,
Satan still tries to find a way!

Lord, I need the strength;
Place me inside Your fist.
Help me to choose the right thing,
When Satan is in the midst.

When Satan brings temptation,
When I feel His grip on me.
Lord, please give me the courage;
To get down on my knees!

Prayer can solve whatever it is,
That Satan attempts to do.
Prayer is also the only way that...
SATAN WILL FLEE FROM YOU!

WRITE A LETTER TO GOD

WRITE A LETTER TO GOD; JUST TO GIVE HIM PRAISE. I WROTE A LETTER TO GOD; NOW, I WRITE ONE EVERYDAY.

WRITE A LETTER TO GOD

Write a letter to God;
It's the way that I pray.
Write a letter to God;
Say what you want to say.

Write a letter to God;
Concentrate on every line.
Write a letter to God;
Tell Him what's on your mind.

Write a letter to God;
"Dear Lord," is how you start.
Write a letter to God;
To Him, pour out your heart.

Write a letter to God;
Thank Him for His Son.
Write a letter to God;
Thank Him for what He's done.

Write a letter to God;
Just to give Him praise.
I wrote a letter to God;
NOW, I WRITE ONE EVERYDAY.

STRUGGLING

I'M CRYING OUT TO YOU OH LORD, PLEASE WIPE AWAY MY TEARS!

STRUGGLING

Lord, You know my heart;
Even better than I do.
I'm tired Lord, my spirit is weak;
Please talk to me, for a few.

Let me hear Your voice,
Wrap me in Your arms.
Place Your shield upon me,
Keep me from all harm.

Lord, please give me some peace.
Lord, please give me some rest.
Put my mind at ease;
Take my troubles off my chest.

Lord, please speak to me;
Just whisper in my ear.
I'm crying out to You, Oh Lord;
PLEASE WIPE AWAY MY TEARS!

HE'S REAL

Last night I dreamed about a Man;
A Man I could not see.
Yet, every step I'd take in life;
This Man would take with me.

When things get hard,
When times are rough; In Jesus' Name I pray.
Then this Man, whom I can't see,
Washes my troubles away.

He gives me strength and courage;
He pulls me through, when I get stuck.
Even when I've fallen,
I find that He's there to pick me up.

Oh what a Friend, an invisible Friend;
Yet, One who is always there.
I believe in Him with all of my heart,
And, I thank Him in every prayer.

For this dream that I had, was not a dream.
In fact, this Man is true;
He's Jesus Christ and if you believe,
JUST PRAY, HE'LL WORK FOR YOU.

HYPOCRITE

How can someone preach to me,
If his life isn't right?
How can someone teach the Word,
If he doesn't know Jesus Christ?

How can I be shown the light,
By someone who can't see?
How can someone remove a speck from my eye,
When in his eye, there's a tree?

How can someone feed me,
When he hasn't been fed himself?
How can someone quench my thirst,
When he's never been to the well.

How can someone tell me about price,
When he does not know cost?
How can anyone lead my way,
WHEN HE HIMSELF IS LOST?

SOMEDAY

SOMEDAY, I'M GOING TO FLY; OVER HILLS AND OVER MOUNTAINS. SOMEDAY, I'M GOING TO DRINK FROM GOD'S NEVER ENDING FOUNTAIN.

SOMEDAY

Someday, I'll see the world.
Someday, I'll touch the sky.
Someday, I'll surely live in a mansion.
Someday, I'll stand ten feet high.

Someday, I'm going to fly;
Over hills and over mountains.
Someday, I'm going to drink from God's;
Never ending fountain.

Someday, I'll have no more worries.
Someday, I'll have no more fears.
Someday I'm going to meet Jesus.
I JUST HOPE, ON THAT DAY I'M PREPARED.

NOBODY TOLD ME

Somebody told me,
"Be careful today."
Somebody told me,
"There would be trouble in your way."

Somebody told me,
"You can be whatever you choose."
Somebody told me,
"At times you'd be confused."

Somebody told me,
"You could have a great life."
Somebody told me,
"You will pay a great price."

Somebody told me,
"Go and spread your wings."
Somebody told me,
"You are going to do great things."

(Continued)

NOBODY TOLD ME

Somebody told me,
"You are going to go far."
Somebody told me,
"You can win this war."

Somebody told me,
"There's only one way to do it right."
Somebody told me,
"To keep Jesus in your life."

Somebody told me,
"Trust God and you'll see."
Yet, nobody told me,
THINGS WERE GOING TO BE EASY.

BE PATIENT

Dear God, It's hard to be patient;
When there are so many things that I need.
Dear God, It's hard to be patient;
I'm coming to You on my knees.

Dear God, It's hard to be patient;
The first thing that I do is pray.
Dear God, It's hard to be patient;
I need You, right away.

Dear God, It's hard to be patient;
I scream Your name out loud.
Dear God, It's hard to be patient;
I need You God, right now!

Dear God, It's hard to be patient;
I feel like I'm losing my mind.
Dear God, It's hard to be patient;
EVEN THOUGH, YOU'RE ALWAYS ON TIME.

BLESS MY HOME

LORD, BLESS THIS HOUSE; BLESS EACH AND EVERY MEMBER. LORD, BLESS EVERY WALL; BLESS EVERYONE WHO MAY ENTER.

BLESS MY HOME

Lord, bless this house;
Bless each and every member.
Lord, bless every wall;
Bless everyone who may enter.

Lord, bless every rug,
Every bed and every stand.
Lord, bless every cup,
Every dish and every pan.

Lord, bless each appliance,
Every couch and every door.
Lord, bless every brick,
Every nail and every board.

Lord, bless every mirror,
Every window and every glass.
Lord, bless everything,
From my ceiling to my trash.

(Continued)

BLESS MY HOME

Lord, bless my dog,
Bless my bird and bless my cat.
Lord, bless my property,
From the front yard to the back.

Lord, bless all of the little things,
That is just not on my brain.
Lord, I ask these blessings of You,
IN JESUS' NAME!

ARE YOU PLANTED?

THINK OF YOURSELF AS A TREE, ARE YOU PLANTED? ARE YOUR ROOTS GOOD? HAVE YOU EVER THOUGHT OF YOUR CHILDREN AS FRUIT? IF NOT, MAYBE NOW YOU SHOULD.

ARE YOU PLANTED?

A tree, whose roots have not been planted;
Its fruit won't grow at all.
In fact, if its roots have not been planted,
The tree itself will fall.

If a tree is planted,
But that trees roots aren't good;
Then when that tree bears fruit,
That trees fruit could be bad too.

Think of yourself as a tree, are you planted?
Are your roots good?
Have you ever thought of your children as fruit?
If not, maybe now you should.

In the past,
I was a tree whose roots had not been planted.
I'd produced fruit that I loved,
But at times I couldn't understand them.

(Continued)

ARE YOU PLANTED?

The fruit that I've produced, I want to grow.
To become much better trees.
But first they must be planted;
Remember, their roots all came from me.

Since I've been planted and accepted Christ,
My roots have grown in the Lord.
It fills my heart with joy to know,
That my fruit will grow so much more.

Someday each of my fruit will be a tree.
Able to bear fruit, but they'll know;
That they must plant their roots somewhere,
If they want their fruit to grow.

ARE YOU PLANTED?

A BROTHER

How can I say that I love my brother,
When I know that a brother is in need?
Every time I refuse to help someone,
A blessing is lost, that God had for me.

A brother is in jail, a brother is on the streets;
A brother is strung out on drugs,
He's cheating on his wife; he's robbing someone.
Yet, I still must show a brother love.

A brother can't be trusted; he's a liar and a thief.
A brother is lost in his ways.
Whatever it takes, I must get to a brother;
Proving Satan to be a liar today!

Lord, I need You today; It's not about me.
There is a brother out there that needs help.
I must remember the words that Jesus once spoke,
"Love your brother, as you love yourself."

No man is perfect; I've been down myself.
Things could be a lot worse, most will agree.
I just pray to God, if I were in another brother's shoes;
THAT A BROTHER WOULD REACH OUT TO ME.

ONE ANSWER

All of my life I thought I knew
The answers to it all.
Yet, every time that I've tried to climb;
I seemed to take a fall.

I've searched and searched, read many books.
Asked friends, but they don't know.
I want to do the right thing,
But which way do I go?

I find it easy to do wrong.
Why is right so hard to do?
When I think I've found the answers,
I find that I did not have a clue.

Trying to find the answers to
The questions I don't know.
Seemed like planting a tree without using dirt,
Then expecting that tree to grow.

(Continued)

ONE ANSWER

Then one night I found the strength,
To get down on my knees.
I prayed to God and what happened next;
Was too good to believe!

I realized there was one book,
That I somehow never read.
I searched for and found this book in a drawer,
Beside my bed.

The Bible was the key,
To everything that I'd ever dreamed.
It let me know that I must believe,
And, get on Jesus team!

He'll secure the way to the top,
As well as help me climb.
I found that He is the only way,
That victory can be mine!

So now when I'm confused,
I know that God is there on call.
If I just pray in Jesus' Name,
NO LONGER WILL I FALL.

SAVED

Dear Lord, I am a sinner.
Please, come into my life today.
Forgive me for my sins,
Listen as I pray.

I believe in Jesus Christ,
Your one and only Son.
Born of the Virgin Mary,
From Bethlehem He comes.

I believe that He died on Calvary.
Crucified, nailed to a cross.
He did this to save us all from sin,
Because we all were lost!

I believe that after He died;
He rose again, alive in three days.
I accept Jesus Christ as my Lord and my Savior.
I BELIEVE THEREFORE, I AM SAVED!

I'M DESPERATE

Lord, I'm messing up;
I'm in a bind again.
There's nowhere else for me to turn,
I need Your help my Friend.

I haven't been a good servant;
Sometimes, I forget to pray.
I haven't been reading my Bible;
Yet, I need You today.

I know that I've let You down,
I'm sorry but I'm in need.
I promise, I'll give You all of the praise;
If You'll just rescue me!

I should have been more careful.
I should have given You more time.
I should have been talking to You everyday;
Not, just when I'm in a bind.

Maybe, You'll still help me?
I'm down Lord, on both knees.
Forgive me for my sins, Oh Lord
CAN YOU HELP ME, PLEASE?

I'M GOING TO TALK TO GOD

I'M GOING TO TALK TO GOD, WHEN I FIRST GET OUT OF BED. I'M GOING TO TALK TO GOD, THAT'S THE FIRST THOUGHT IN MY HEAD.

I'M GOING TO TALK TO GOD

I'm going to talk to God,
When I first get out of bed.
I'm going to talk to God,
That's the first thought in my head.

I'm going to talk to God,
When I'm as happy as I can be.
I'm going to talk to God,
When something great has happened to me.

I'm going to talk to God,
Every time I need a friend.
I'm going to talk to God,
To ask forgiveness for my sins.

I'm going to talk to God,
When everything is great.
I'm going to talk to God,
Especially when I've made mistakes.

Even when I'm down and out,
When things aren't going my way;
I'm still going to get down on both knees,
AND, TALK TO GOD TODAY!

HE CAN

In the beginning, God created...

Heaven and Earth

In the beginning, God formed man from...

Dirt

In the beginning, God took a rib from...

Man

In the beginning, God took that rib and made...

Woman

In the beginning, God created the...

Land and the Sea

Now ask yourself one question,

"WHAT CAN'T GOD DO FOR ME?"

ME

I am who God created,

From my head down to my toe.

He gave me my brain, He gave me my heart;

He causes my blood to flow.

My body is not my body,

It is a temple of God.

I am responsible for what enters it,

Being careful is a full time job.

I am a Child of God,

This I must understand.

I must keep praising and thanking Him,

PUTTING EVERYTHING INTO HIS HANDS.

CALL ON JESUS

Who can I count on,
When I feel abused?
Who can I count on,
When I've got bad news?

Who can I count on,
When my life is a mess?
Who can I count on,
When there's no one else left?

Who can I count on,
When I'm sick or when I'm weak?
Who can I count on,
Who can I seek?

Why not call on Jesus?
If I give the Lord a chance.
Why not call on Jesus?
If I place it in God's hands.

(Continued)

CALL ON JESUS

Why not call on Jesus?
If I get down on my knees.
Why not call on Jesus?
If I just say, "Lord God, please!"

Why not call on Jesus?
If I trust that He's my Friend.
Why not call on Jesus?
WHY? BECAUSE I'LL FIND OUT THAT HE CAN.

MORNING PRAYER

Good Morning Lord,
Thank you Jesus, You woke me up again.
If in my sleep I have let You down,
Please forgive me for my sin.

Lead me through this day,
Help me to stay strong.
Guide my every step,
That I may resist doing wrong.

Keep me in perfect health,
Supply my every need.
Let my attitude be kind,
Let Your light shine bright in me.

Lord, just take my hand,
Guide me and have Your way.
Help me to be a better me,
IN JESUS' NAME I PRAY!

PREPARATION

Lord, please give me strength,
Satan is on the attack.
Lord, give me the courage,
To stop Him in His tracks!

Lord, I ask your blessings,
Provide me with what I need.
Lord, if it will be Your will,
I know that I'll succeed.

Lord, give me the wisdom,
To make the right decisions.
Lord, please help me to understand,
Open my ears, to help me listen.

Lord, it's not my fight,
The battle belongs to You.
I just ask, in Jesus' Name;
DEAR LORD, PLEASE PULL ME THROUGH!

IT'S ALL GOOD

I have ups, I have downs,

I have good times, and bad;

Yet, through everything

My heart is always glad.

Since I have found Christ,

Since I've accepted Him as my Savior.

Everything is changing in me;

My moods, attitudes, and my behaviors.

I'm just not myself anymore,

I really don't want to be.

I have joy in all of my circumstances,

Because of Christ who lives in me.

I'm learning not to worry,

I have peace in my life today.

Hallelujah thank You Jesus,

That's all that I can say!

IT'S ALL GOOD!

Isaiah 26:3 He will keep you in perfect peace whose mind is stayed on Him.

THANK YOU, LORD

Lord, I can't say enough,

You have blessed me is so many ways.

Most of which I don't deserve,

I must give You some praise.

Without You, I am nothing;

Because of You, I am.

I love You Lord,

I must say thanks for You created man.

In You, I put my trust.

In You, I shall believe.

In You, I'll find my strength.

Because of You, I will succeed.

Thank you for Your blessings.

Thank you for Your love.

Thank you for Your Son.

Thank you for His blood

Thank you Lord for everything,

You've been so good to me.

You've blessed me Lord, in so many ways;

EVEN WAYS THAT I CAN'T SEE.

THANKS

Thank you for reading my poems,
And, may they be a blessing to all readers.
I pray that through my poems,
God will touch you in a mighty way.

I ask that you please continue to pray,
And, trust in the Lord.
He is able to move mountains in your life.
Just like He has done in mine.

THANKS AGAIN!

May God Bless and Keep You.

TO GOD BE THE GLORY!

www.ingramcontent.com/pod-product-compliance
Lightning Source LLC
Chambersburg PA
CBHW031300290426
44109CB00012B/655